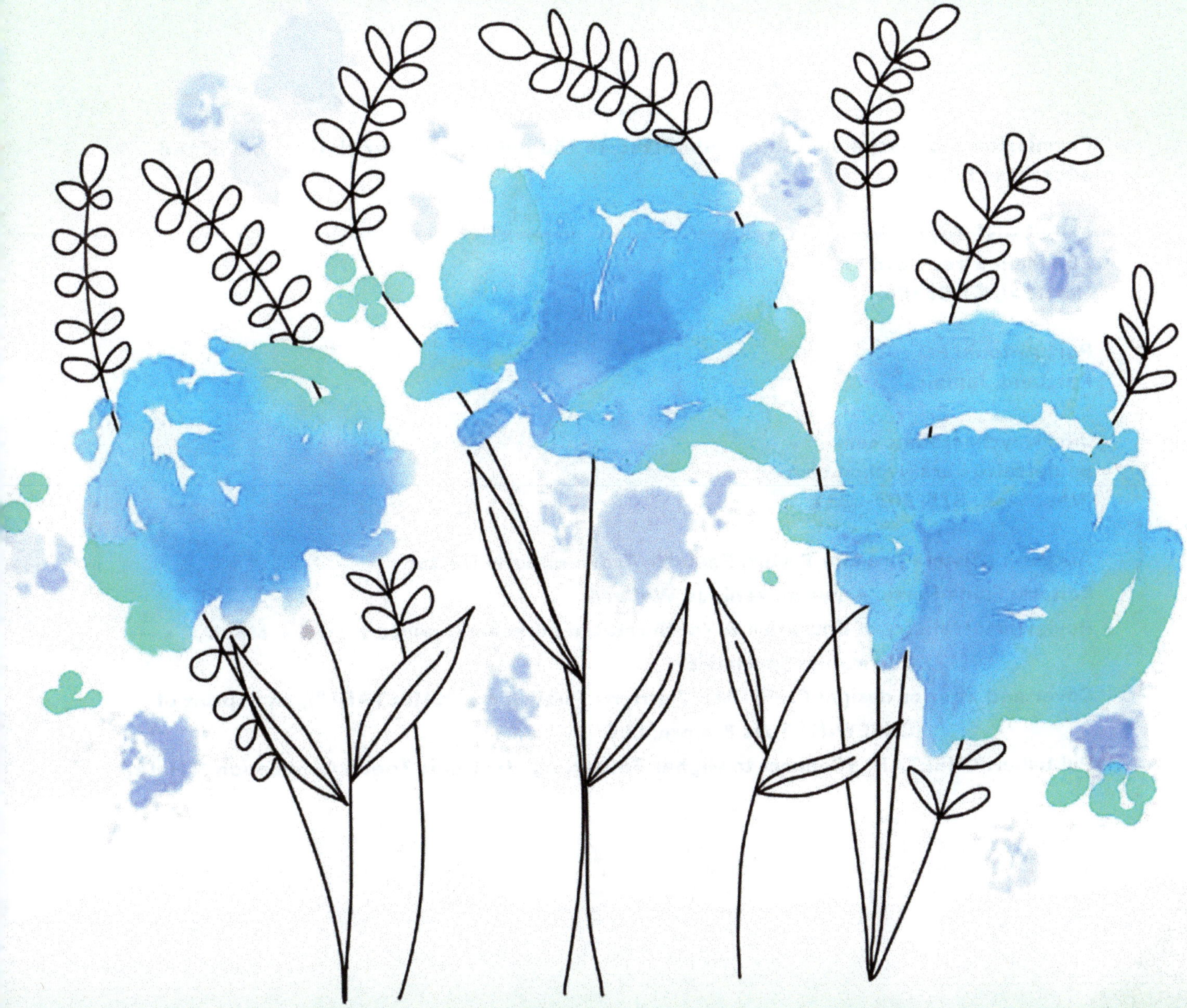

10 9 8 7 6 5 4 3 2 1

Copyright© 2024 by CHEETAH® Toys & More, LLC.

No part of this publication may be reproduced, distributed, or transmitted in any form or by any means, including photocopying, recording, or other electronic or mechanical methods, without the prior written permission of the publisher, except in the case of brief quotations embodied in critical reviews and certain other non-commercial uses permitted by copyright law.

Although every precaution has been taken to verify the accuracy of the information contained herein, the author and publisher assume no responsibility for any errors or omissions. No liability is assumed for damages that may result from the use of information contained within. Your legal remedy, if any, is limited to the amount paid for this book and/or training.

Permission request(s) should be submitted to the publisher in writing at one of the addresses below:

CHEETAH® Toys & More, LLC
207 Main Street, 3rd Floor
Hartford, CT 06106

Port Antonio PO
Portland, Jamaica

info@mycheetahinc.com
paulettetrowers@yahoo.com
WhatsApp: 876-909-6311

Authors: Kristina Jaz; Iain Taylor; Paulette Trowers, Juris Doctor
Editors: Fiona Porter-Lawson; Yanique Wallace
Reviewers: Ministry of Education & Youth related personnel; Janice Trowers, MSED, Curriculum Specialist
Cover and interior design: CHEETAH® Purrrrrrr Publishing ("CHEETAH®"), an imprint of CHEETAH® Toys & More, LLC.
Publisher: CHEETAH® (Connect to Higher Education, Electronic Tools, Application & Help)

This book belongs to:

Name:

....

School:

....

Date:

....

Table of Contents

Dear CHEETAH family, — 2

Set 6: ng, w, short oo, long oo, v — 4

Set 7: ch, sh, long e, th and y — 28

Set 8: x, qu, oi, long u, and ar — 52

Set 9: ow, ou, er, soft c and zh — 78

I am LaChase, a cheetah, reader and future leader. I want to introduce you to my friend, Hooty Hoot. Come with me. Let's go, let's go.

Dear CHEETAH family,

As you teach each sound, the lesson format will follow the CHEETAH® CAPE tool.

CONCEPT (exploration) sections give the information and knowledge the pupil needs to understand the lesson fully. Look at the letter that represents the phonic sound and practise making the sound together. Use the story and its action to hear the letter sound in context. Show the pupil where the phonic sound can appear in a word. Say the words in the word bank together and use the story to find more words with the focus sound.

Teach me and I will learn.

> This symbol shows sections to be read by the adult.
> Using instruments and the CHEETAH train song lyrics is another way for auditory learners to further explore the sound.

APPLY (elaboration) sections ask the pupil to apply the information they have learned to solve problems.

Show me and I will follow.

PRACTICE (further elaboration) sections allow the pupil to use the information and skills they have learned during fun activities that are guided by the teacher.

Let me do it and I will not forget.

EVALUATE (self-reflection) sections are a chance for the teacher and parent to communicate and keep track of the pupil's understanding of key concepts. Pupils get a chance to express their feelings. This is also where the pupil, parent or guardian will be given stickers to celebrate their learning!

How am I doing?

Clusters for Teaching Phonemes*

Week 1: s, (short) a, m, (short) e, p

Week 2: f, n, (short) i, t, r

Week 3: d, (short) o, g, h, c/k

Week 4: l, b, (short) u, g, (long) a

Week 5: j, (long) i, or, (long) o, z

Week 6: ng, w/wh, oo/oo, v

Week 7: ch, sh, (long) e, th(voiced), th(unvoiced), y

Week 8: x, qu, oi, (long) u, ar

Week 9: ow/ou, zh, er

*As provided by MOEY.

**Throughout our books, we substituted 'week' for 'set'

Set 6

ng, /w/, short oo, long oo and /v/

Here are some JamDER books to read:

Sound	JamDER reference	Book title
ng	Set 2, Book 14	*Going Shopping*
w	Set 3, Book 19	*Where is Willie?*
long oo	Set 1, Book 6	*I Like School*

5+

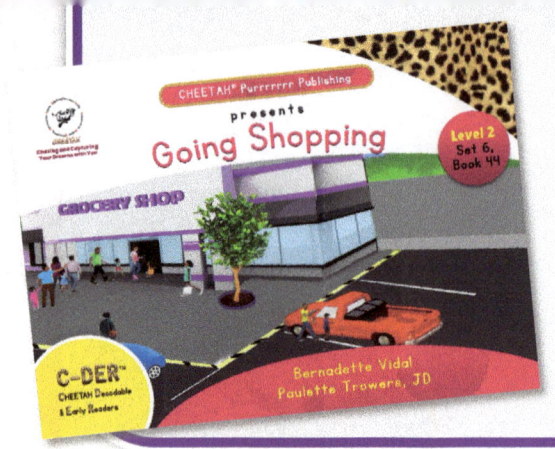

Let's read together: Going Shopping

Before you begin, allow the child to be the teacher! Ask, "What questions would a teacher ask about this book?"

During the story ask, "How does Sam feel when he sees the car? How does he feel when his dad says he can't have the car?

After the story ask, "Can you list the things the family bought?" Encourage the child to look back through the story.

CHEETAH® train loves a song, zooming as it hums along. Eating mango in her seat, Pam dances to a jungle beat. Can you guess which sound is next?

Find an instrument, then play and sing along using the lyrics above!

Our sound is sent through your nose!

NG is on the way to town.
CHEETAH® train is slowing down.

Read and (circle) the /ng/ word that matches the picture.

ng

sing

ring

wing

ping

hang

bang

Practise writing the letters *n* and *g*.

You can do this!

ng ng ng

Listen and underline all the words in the passage with /ng/ sound.

At school, we learned about the lungs.

"What are they for?" my friend asked.

"They take in air and help us to sing," the teacher said.

"Taking care of them is a very important thing."

Colour the face that shows how you feel about the /ng/ sound.

😊 Got it!   😐 Almost got it   ☹ No, didn't get it

Keep working hard!

Dear Parent: Date: _____

_____ does/does not fully understand the phonic sound /ng/. Please continue to review at home.

Signed: _____

Dear Teacher: Date:_____

Thank you. We have reviewed the phonic sound /ng/ together. My child had a chance to teach me.

Signed: _____

Reward sticker for parent or guardian goes here.

Great job!

_____
(write name)

understands the phonic sound /ng/.

Sticker for pupil goes here!

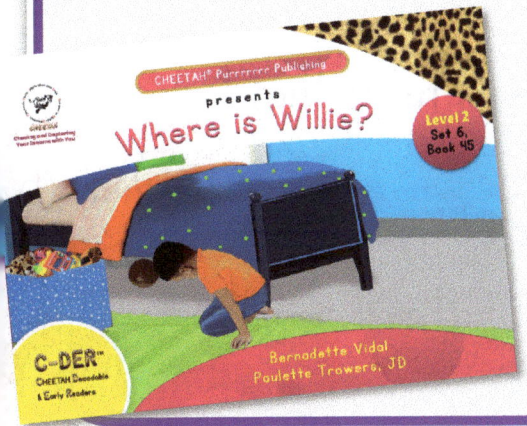

Let's read together: Where is Willie?

Before you begin ask, "Who do you think Willie might be? What do you think has happened to them?"

During the story, stop once or twice to ask, "Where has Ben looked for Willie so far? Where could he look next?"

After the story ask, "Can you tell me what happened in the story? Was Willie who you expected him to be?"

CHEETAH® train loves a song, zooming as it hums along. A whale washes while he swims. He knows that we are watching him. Can you guess which sound is next?

Find an instrument, then play and sing along using the lyrics above!

Move your lips to make our sound!

WH is on the way to town.
CHEETAH® train is slowing down.

Listen as an adult says the words. Colour the pictures that have the /w/ sound.

Ww
wh

Practise writing the letters *w* and *h*.

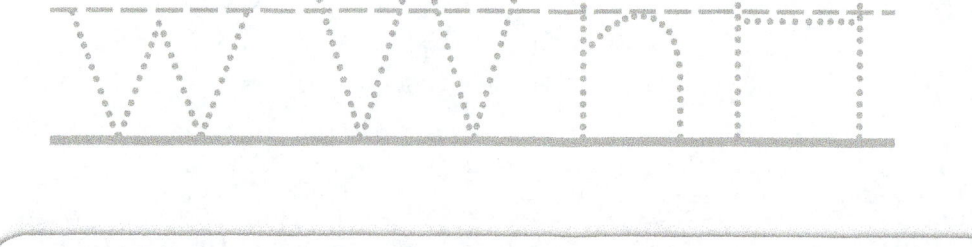

I am so proud of you!

Listen and colour all the words in the passage with /w/ sound brown.

The worm had a wish on a windy Wednesday.

"I wish to win a ride on a whale" he did say.

"Well, hop on!" said the whale in the bay.

The worm was happy, and they swam away.

Colour the face that shows how you feel about the /w/ sound.

😊 Got it!   😐 Almost got it   ☹️ No, didn't get it

You are doing great! Keep going.

Dear Parent: Date: _____

_____ does/does not fully understand the phonic sound /w/. Please continue to review at home.

Signed: _____

Dear Teacher: Date:_____

Thank you. We have reviewed the phonic sound /w/ together. . My child had a chance to teach me.

Signed: _____

Reward sticker for parent or guardian goes here.

Wonderful!

_____
(write name

understands the phonic sound /w/.

Sticker for pupil goes here!

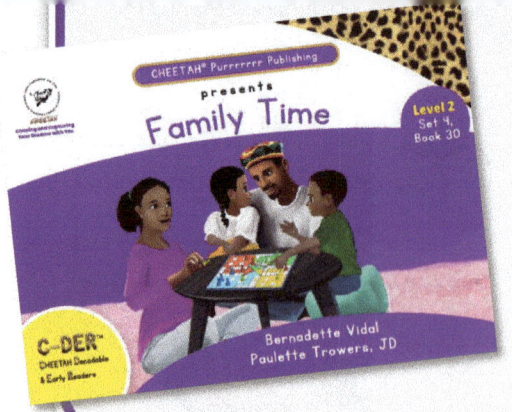

Let's read together: Family Time

Before you begin ask, "*What does this picture tell you about this family? How is this family the same as /different to yours?*"

During the story, stop at page 11. Ask, "*How does this image help to show us what sap is?*"

After the story, encourage the child to read the story out loud to you, correctly using the conventions of print (directionality, return sweep).

CHEETAH® train loves a song, zooming as it hums along. Look, a rook with James the cook! James is reading books beside the brook. Can you guess which sound is next?

Find an instrument, then play and sing along using the lyrics above!

What shape are your lips as you make my sound?

O is on the way to town.
CHEETAH® train is slowing down.

Say the words. Circle all the pictures with the short /oo/ sound.

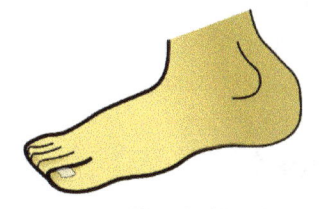

oo

Practise writing the letter O.

You are doing great!

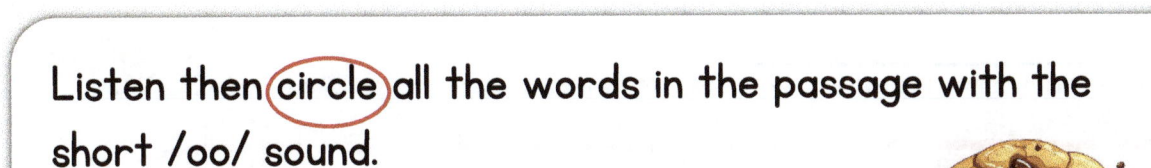

Listen then circle all the words in the passage with the short /oo/ sound.

At school, I took a look in my nook.

"Oh no! Where is my book?" I said.

"It is under the wood," said my good friend Brook.

I was so happy; I gave him a cookie I had cooked.

Colour the face that shows how you feel about the short /oo/ sound.

😊 Got it!   😐 Almost got it   ☹ No, didn't get it

Don't give up. You are doing great!

Dear Parent: Date: _____

_____ does/does not fully understand the short /oo/ sound. Please continue to review at home.

Signed: _____

Dear Teacher: Date: _____

Thank you. We have reviewed the phonic sound short /oo/ together. My child had a chance to teach me.

Signed: _____

Reward sticker for parent or guardian goes here.

Good work!

_____
(write name)

understands the phonic sound short /oo/.

Sticker for pupil goes here!

Let's read together: I Like School

Before you begin ask, "Do you like school? What do you like/dislike about it?"

During the story, encourage the child to read along when able, using the conventions of print (directionality and return sweep).

After the story ask, "Did you learn any new words reading this story? Can you separate these new words into phonemes?"

CHEETAH® train loves a song, zooming as it hums along. Baboons board the CHEETAH Train! Soon we're zooming off again. Can you guess which sound is next?

Find an instrument, then play and sing along using the lyrics above!

Look in a mirror as you make my sound!

O is on the way to town.
CHEETAH® train is slowing down.

Read the words out loud. Draw lines to match the word to the picture.

Oo

spoon   zoo   moon   broom

Practise writing the letter O.

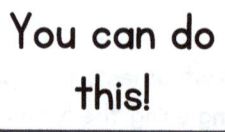

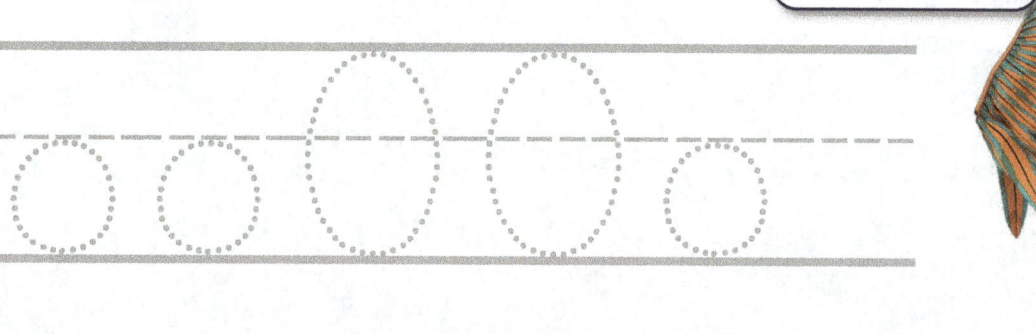

You can do this!

Listen and underline all the words in the passage with the long /oo/ sound.

The goose waits on the stoop for racoon.
They have a plan to eat noodles.
She sweeps the stoop while she waits.
The goose hopes raccoon will get here soon.

Colour the face that shows how you feel about the phonic sound long /oo/.

🙂 Got it!   😐 Almost got it   ☹️ No, didn't get it

Keep trying and you will succeed!

Dear Parent:　　　　　Date: _____

_____ does/does not fully understand the phonic sound long /oo/. Please continue to review at home.

Signed: _____

Dear Teacher:　　　　　Date:_____

Thank you. We have reviewed the phonic sound long /oo/ together. My child had a chance to teach me.

Signed: _____

Reward sticker for parent or guardian goes here.

Fantastic!

_____
(write name)

understands the phonic sound long /oo/.

Sticker for pupil goes here!

Let's read together: Vacation Time

Before you begin ask, *"What is a vacation? Have you ever been on vacation?"*

During the story, look for picture clues and words that fit the context of a vacation. List the words found.

After the story, use the words found to write sentences about being on vacation.

CHEETAH® train loves a song, zooming as it hums along. A dove is flying very high. She loves to dive around the sky. Can you guess which sound is next?

Find an instrument, then play and sing along using the lyrics above!

Where do you place your teeth to make my sound?

V is on the way to town.
CHEETAH® train is slowing down.

Rearrange the letters to write the /v/ sound words.

_ _ _ _
v e c a

_ _ _ _
e v f i

_ _ _
a n v

Practise writing the letter V.

Very good work!

Listen then underline all the words in the passage with the /v/ sound.

In the village, everyone loves vegetables.

Violet loves avocados and olives.

She makes a salad with seven olives and five avocados.

The village families love to eat it!

Vv

Colour the face that shows how you feel about the /v/ sound.

😊 Got it!   😐 Almost got it   ☹️ No, didn't get it

Spread your wings and keep flying!

Dear Parent: Date: _____

_____ does/does not fully understand the phonic sound /v/. Please continue to review at home.

Signed: _____

Dear Teacher: Date:_____

Thank you. We have reviewed the phonic sound /v/ together. My child had a chance to teach me.

Signed: _____

Reward sticker for parent or guardian goes here.

Marvelous!

_____
(write name)

understands the phonic sound /v/.

Sticker for pupil goes here!

CHEETAH®'s review

Write four words from the word box that rhyme. Cross out the words you use.

1. _____   2. _____

3. _____   4. _____

Write four words from the word box that rhyme. Cross out the words you use.

1. _____   2. _____

3. _____   4. _____

Write two words from the word bank that rhyme.

1. _____   2. _____

Word Box

sing

hoop

took

wing

look

ring

loop

book

king

hook

Write a sentence with a word from the word box. Remember to start your sentence with a capital letter and end with punctuation! (. ? !)

_____

Use the letters to make as many words as you can.

ng   k   g
  oo   i
b   t   l

CHEETAH®'s review

Find the high frequency words in the wordsearch.

w	h	y	o	w
h	o	h	y	h
i	w	u	w	e
c	h	e	l	n
h	o	l	i	d

would   who   when   which   why

Choose 6 of this set's CHEETAH sight word cards. Number them 1-6. Roll a dice. Look at the card with that number, cover it up, write it out, then check if your spelling is correct.

Which letters can you add to the *oon* word family?

<u>s</u>oon   ___oon   ___oon   ___oon

Make a word family using letters *ng*.

<u>s</u>ing   ___ng   ___ng   _____   _____

The Whale and the Book

A CHEETAH® Poster Story

ng, w/wh, oo/OO, v

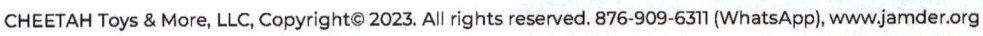

1. This is Vick and his pal, a whale. 
2. Vick and the whale play. Ping! 
3. The whale and Vick ride a wave. 
4. Vick will ring a bell with his wing. 
5. Ding, ding! Ring the white bell! 
6. The whale will sing to Vick.

The Whale and the Book

A CHEETAH® Poster Story

Set 6

ng, w/wh, oo/OO, v

7. Look! There is a book on the wave!

8. Look at Vick dive for the book! Zing!

9. The whale can dive too! Zoom!

10. Will the whale hook the book?

11. The whale did save the book. But the book is wet.

12. Vick read the book to the whale. The book is good!

13. The whale and Vick wave to the moon.

CHEETAH Toys & More, LLC, Copyright© 2023. All rights reserved. 876-909-6311 (WhatsApp), www.jamder.org

JamDER™
Jamaican Decodable & Early Readers

23

Let's create

Complete the table. Put the letters together to make words.

beginning sound	middle sound	end sound	words created
wh w v	a e i o u	t g p r ng	

List the words that you do not know the meaning of.

_____

_____

Ask an adult what they mean.

Let's put together

Connect the boxes to make words from the -ook word family. Write them in the given space.

b
c   _ook   _____
h   _____
t   _____
                    _____

Seeing patterns in words helps us to learn them.

Let's take apart

Break each word into sounds. Write the letters that make each sound.

Say the word and listen to the sounds.

Let's trace

Trace the letters to write sentences.

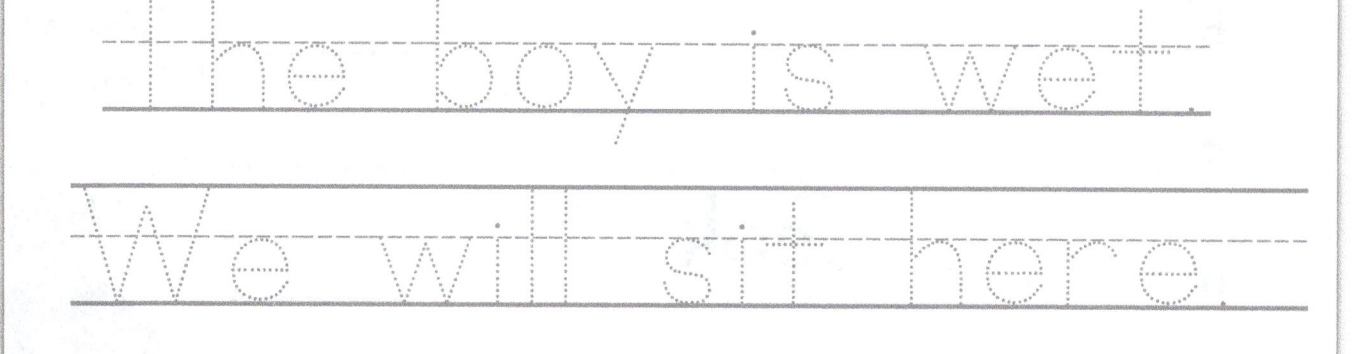

The boy is wet.

We will sit here.

Read the sentences you have written.

CHEETAH® reward stickers

This page is left blank
so you can cut out the reward
stickers.

Set 7

ch, sh, long e, th and y

Here are some JamDER books to read:

Sound	JamDER reference	Book title
ch	Set 5, Book 39	*Beach Time*
sh	Set 5, Book 39	*I Wish*
long e	Set 4, Book 30	*Mr. Pete*
th	Set 2, Book 17	*Who's There?*

5+

Set 7: ch, sh, long e, th and y

Let's read together: Beach Time

Before you begin ask, *"How would you prepare for beach time? What do you think the characters might do at the beach?"*

During the story, stop when the crab is seen. Ask, *"How does Sam/Bella feel when they see the crab? How do you know?"*

After the story ask, *"Did Sam and Bella have a good time at the beach? How do you know?"*

CHEETAH® train loves a song, zooming as it hums along.
Charlie Chicken chews on cheese. At lunchtime he is very pleased!
Can you guess which sound is next?

Find an instrument, then play and sing along using the lyrics above!

Make a burst of air to make our sound!

CH is on the way to town.
CHEETAH® train is slowing down.

Draw lines to match each word to the correct picture.

church   cheese   chair   beach

ch

Practise writing the letters *c* and *h*.

Cheers!

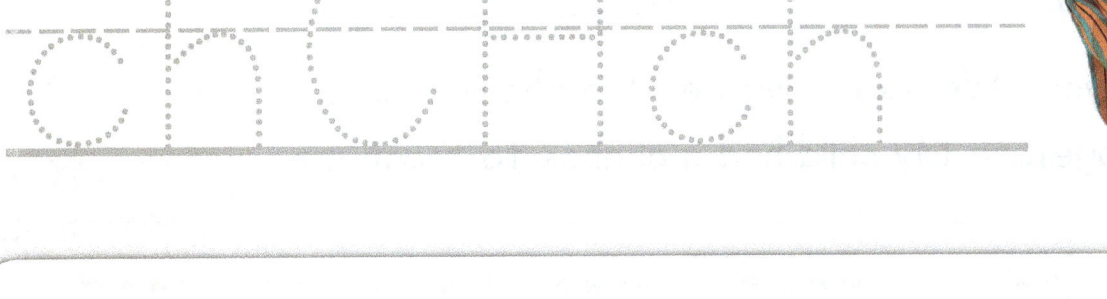

Listen and underline all the words in the passage with the /ch/ sound.

At the beach, there was a big chess match.

But two children nearby were playing catch.

"Careful with that ball!" the teacher said.

The children stopped playing and watched chess instead.

Colour the face that shows how you feel about the /ch/ sound.

Got it! Almost got it No, didn't get it

Practise makes perfect! Challenge yourself and try the section again.

Dear Parent: Date: _____

_____ does/does not fully understand the phonic sound /ch/. Please continue to review at home.

Signed: _____

Dear Teacher: Date:_____

Thank you. We have reviewed the phonic sound /ch/ together. My child had a chance to teach me.

Signed: _____

Reward sticker for parent or guardian goes here.

Well done!

_____
(write name

understands the phonic sound /ch/.

Sticker for pupil goes here!

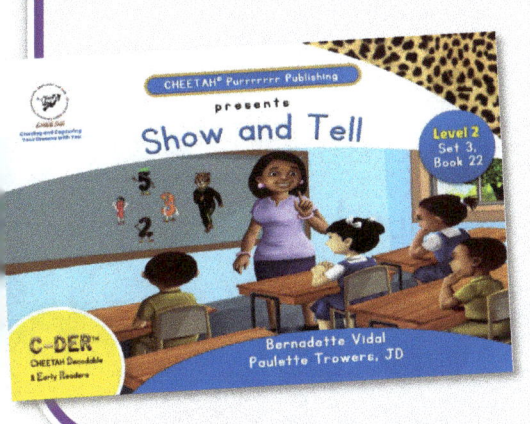

Let's read together: Show and Tell

Before you begin ask, "What is show and tell? What would you bring to show and tell? Why would you choose this?"

During the story ask, "When did we see Willie before? What happened to him? Do you think he will get lost in this story?"

After the story ask, "What did each character bring to show and tell? Which was your favourite? Why?"

CHEETAH® train loves a song, zooming as it hums along. Sheep are sleeping in the shade, wearing shoes the shepherd made. Can you guess which sound is next?

Find an instrument, then play and sing along using the lyrics above!

Look in a mirror as you make our sound!

SH is on the way to town.
CHEETAH® train is slowing down.

(Circle) all the pictures that contain the /sh/ sound.

Practise writing the letters *s* and *h*.

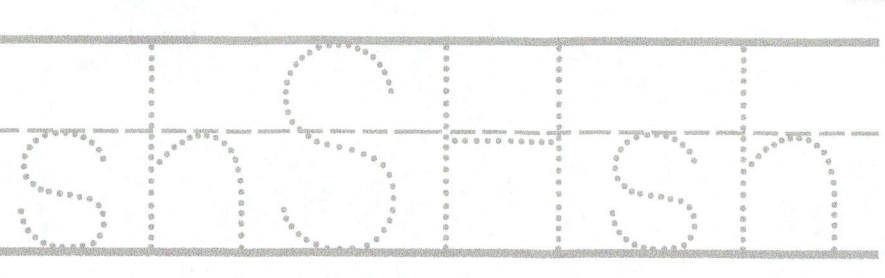

sh sh sh

Keep up the good job!

Listen and underline all the words in the passage with the /sh/ sound.

Shelly has shiny shoes that she loves to show.

She wears them to the shop and in the snow.

"Look at my shoes!" she shouts with glee.

"They shine so bright, just like me!"

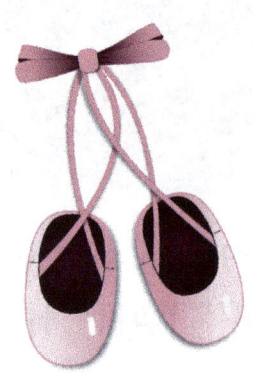

sh

Colour the face that shows how you feel about the sh sound.

You are doing well. Keep practising.

Got it!   Almost got it   No, didn't get it

Dear Parent: Date: _____

_____ does/does not fully understand the phonic sound /sh/. Please continue to review at home.

Signed: _____

Dear Teacher: Date: _____

Thank you. We have reviewed the phonic sound /sh/ together. My child had a chance to teach me.

Signed: _____

Reward sticker for parent or guardian goes here.

Great job!

_____
(write name)

understands the phonic sound /sh/.

Sticker for pupil goes here!

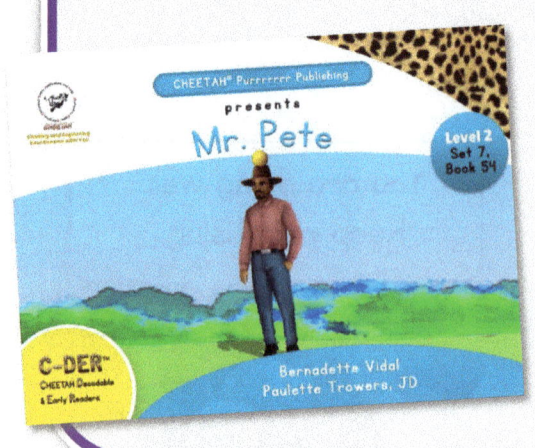

Let's read together: Mr Pete

Before you begin ask, "*What do the title and illustration tell us about the main character in this story?*"

During the story, encourage the child to read the simpler pages or sentences, using fix-up strategies such as reading ahead to help with unknown words.

After the story ask, "*What was the problem in this story? How was the problem solved?*"

CHEETAH® train loves a song, zooming as it hums along. Edith sleeps beside the sea. She sees the train and waves at me! Can you guess which letter sound is next?

Find an instrument, then play and sing along using the lyrics above!

What shape is your mouth as you make my sound?

E is on the way to town.
CHEETAH® train is slowing down.

Colour in the words which are spelt correctly.

bee
bea

grean
green

trea
tree

sea
see

ee
ea

Practise writing the letters *e*.

Keep it up!

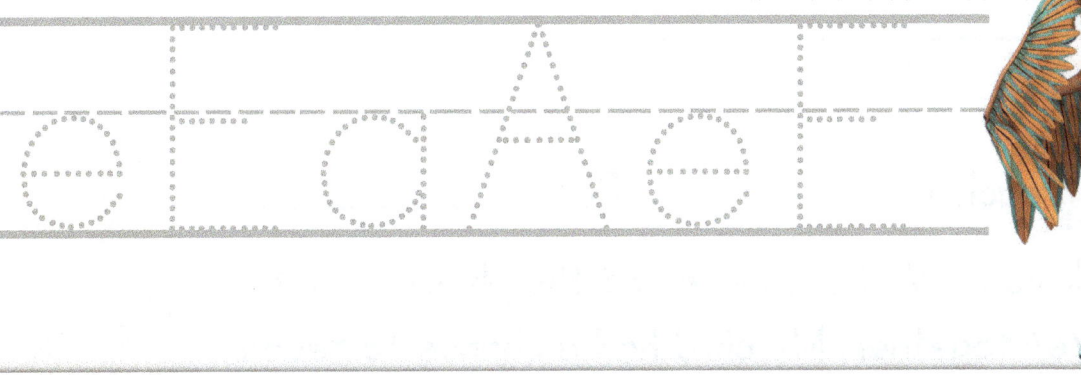

Listen and colour all the words in the passage with the long ē sound green.

Eve the bee loves to fly to the big tree.

She makes sweet honey, as good as tea.

"This tree is best," she said with a smile.

"I will sleep in the tree, just you see!"

Colour the face that shows how you feel about the long /ē/ sound.

Got it! Almost got it No, didn't get it

It is so much fun to learn and play. You are doing great!

Dear Parent: Date: _____

_____ does/does not fully understand the long phonic sound /ē/. Please continue to review at home.

Signed: _____

Dear Teacher: Date:_____

Thank you. We have reviewed the phonic sound long /ē/ together. My child had a chance to teach.

Signed: _____

Reward sticker for parent or guardian goes here.

Incredible!

_____
(write name

understands the phonic sound ē.

Sticker for pupil goes here!

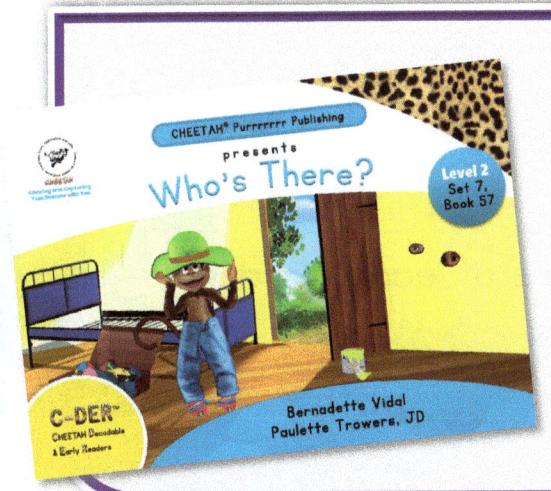

Let's read together: Who's There?

Before you begin ask, *"What is the setting for this story? Who do you think might be in the shed?"*

During the story, encourage the child to read along, using their knowledge of high frequency words and blending phonemes for any words unknown.

After the story ask, *"When have you seen monkey before? Is this how monkey usually behaves?"*

CHEETAH® train loves a song, zooming as it hums along.
Theo and his sister Beth settle down to catch their breath.
Can you guess which sound is next?

Find an instrument, then play and sing along using the lyrics above!

Stick out your tongue to make our sound!

TH is on the way to town.
CHEETAH® train is slowing down.

Read the th words out loud. Draw a picture of each word.

th

mother

path

tooth

Practise writing the letters *t* and *h*.

Take your time. Keep practising!

th th th th

Listen and underline all the words in the passage with the th sound.

"Where is that book that I had?" said Beth.

"Is it the one with the thorny rose on the cover?"

"Yes, that is it!" she said with thanks and a cheer.

"I knew we would find it. That was never a fear"

Colour the face that shows how you feel about the /th/ sound.

Got it! Almost got it No, didn't get it

Do not be afraid to do a section again. Keep practising!

Dear Parent: Date: _____

_____ does/does not fully understand the phonic sound /th/. Please continue to review at home.

Signed: _____

Dear Teacher: Date: _____

Thank you. We have reviewed the phonic sound /th/ together. My child had a chance to teach me.

Signed: _____

Reward sticker for parent or guardian goes here.

Fantastic!

_____
(write name

understands the phonic sound /th/.

Sticker for pupil goes here!

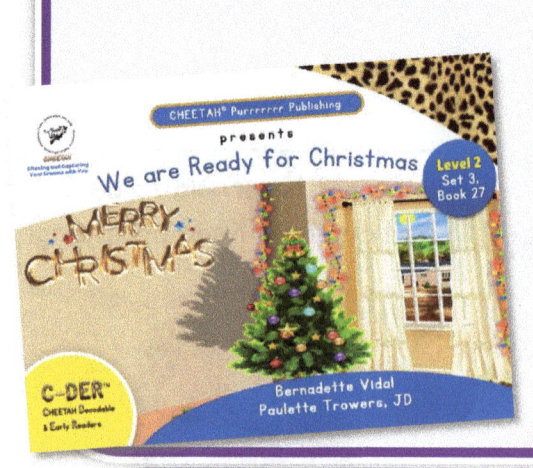

Let's read together: We are Ready for Christmas

Before you begin ask, "What do you think the setting for this story will be? Why do you think that?"

During the story, stop at various points to ask, "How does Cara feel? What tells you this?"

After the story ask, "How did Cara feel at the end of the story? How could you help less fortunate people at Christmas?"

CHEETAH® train loves a song, zooming as it hums along. Yan the Yeti yawns and sleeps. There's yogurt on his yellow teeth. Can you guess which sound is next?

Find an instrument, then play and sing along using the lyrics above!

How does your mouth make my sound?

Y is on the way to town.
CHEETAH® train is slowing down.

Listen as an adult says the words. Tick (✓) the pictures that contain the /y/ sound.

Yy

Practise writing the letter y.

Practice makes perfect!

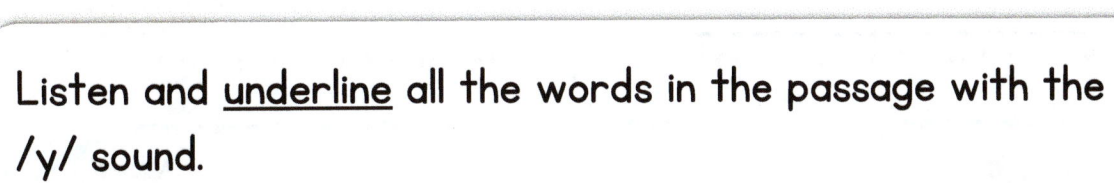

Listen and <u>underline</u> all the words in the passage with the /y/ sound.

Yumi loves to eat yams every day.

She keeps them in the barnyard, they say.

"Yams are so yummy!" she would cry with glee.

"A yam a day, for you and for me!"

Colour the face that shows how you feel about the /y/ sound.

😊 Got it!   😐 Almost got it   ☹ No, didn't get it

Great job! I am very proud of you. Always keep practising!

Dear Parent: Date: _____

_____ does/does not fully understand the phonic sound /y/. Please continue to review at home.

Signed: _____

Dear Teacher: Date:_____

Thank you. We have reviewed the phonic sound /y/ together. My child had a chance to teach me.

Signed: _____

Reward sticker for parent or guardian goes here.

Hooray!

_____
(write name

understands the phonic sound /y/.

Sticker for pupil goes here!

CHEETAH®'s review

Circle all of the words in each row that have the same beginning sound as the picture.

|  chip | whale | beach | chime |

|  wish | chin | shop | shake |

|  think | when | shed | thin |

|  yes | by | yum | eat |

Use the letters to make as many long e words as you can.

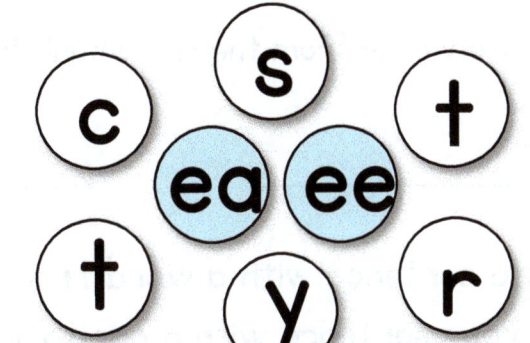

c s t
ea ee
t y r

CHEETAH®'s review

Find the sight words in the wordsearch.

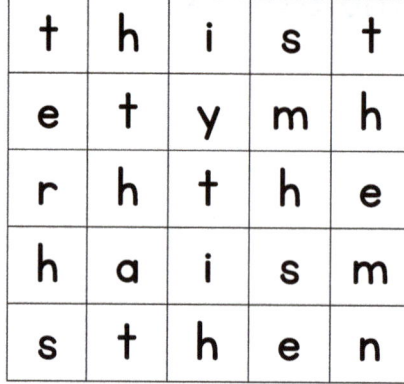

t	h	i	s	t
e	t	y	m	h
r	h	t	h	e
h	a	i	s	m
s	t	h	e	n

them   this   that   then   the

Write four words from the word box that rhyme. Cross out the words you use.

1. _____   2. _____

3. _____   4. _____

Write four words from the word box that rhyme. Cross out the words you use.

1. _____   2. _____

3. _____   4. _____

Write two words from the word bank that rhyme.

1. _____   2. _____

Write a sentence with a word from the word box. Remember to start your sentence with a capital letter and end with punctuation! (. ? !)

_____

Word Box

lash

bean

cash

lean

thin

dash

chin

seen

teen

mash

CHEETAH® Purrrrrrr Publishing
presents
A Yummy Dish

Set 7

ch, sh, long e, th (voiced), th (unvoiced), y

CHEETAH® Poster Story

1. "Dad! Can we cook some yummy food with this book?"

2. "Yes! We will make this yam dish."

3. "Yes. But we will need to shop for more limes."

4. They shop for limes and peas.

5. "Chill the tea in this jug while we cook."

6. "Now, we chop the yam into thin shapes."

CHEETAH Toys & More, LLC, Copyright© 2023.

A Yummy Dish

CHEETAH® Poster Story

7. "You can beat the egg with the chives."

8. We will bake this into chips."

9. "Then make a yam patty. Put the patty in a pan."

10. "Take a seat. I will give this pan some heat."

11. Yum! A yam patty with lime chips!

CHEETAH Toys & More, LLC, Copyright© 2023.

Let's create

Complete the table. Put the letters together to make words.

beginning sound	middle sound	end sound	words created
ch sh th	a e i o u y	t	
		g	
		p	
		r	
		w	
		b	

List the words that you do not know the meaning of.

_____

_____

Ask an adult what they mean.

Let's put together

Connect the boxes to make words from the -eat word family. Write them in the given space.

b
m
s
ch

_eat

_____
_____
_____
_____

Knowing word families will help your spelling.

Let's take apart

Break each word into sounds. Write the sounds in the boxes.

Focus on the letters one sound at a time.

Let's trace

Trace the letters to write sentences.

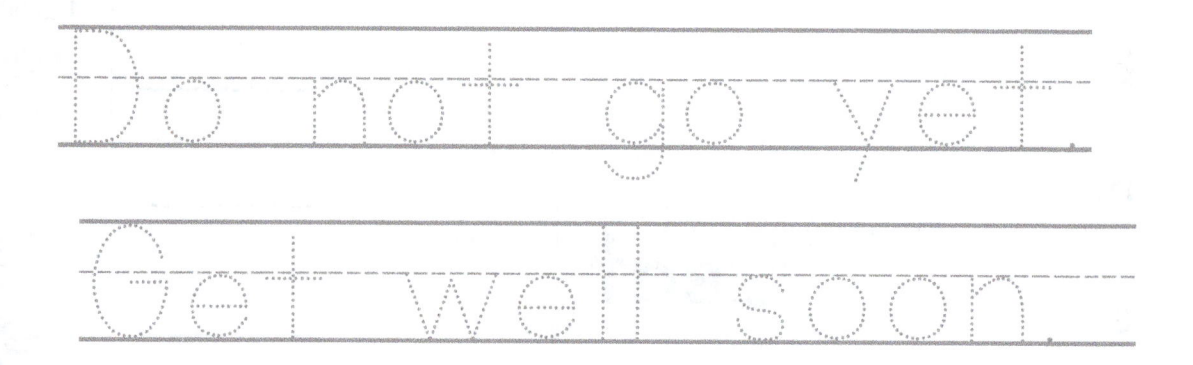

Do not go yet.

Get well soon.

Read the sentences you have written.

CHEETAH® reward stickers

This page is left blank
so you can cut out the reward
stickers.

Set 8

x, qu, oi, long u, and ar

Here are some JamDER books to read:

Sound	JamDER reference	Book title
x	Set 6, Book 46	*Story Time*
qu	Set 7, Book 62	*Do Not Quit*
long u	Set 3, Book 21	*What's Cooking?*

Set 8: /x/, /qu/, /oi/, long /u/ and /ar/

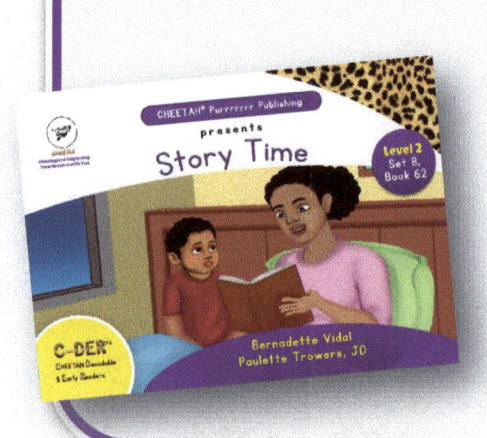

Let's read together: Story Time

Before you begin ask, "Do you have a time to read stories? What types of stories do you like to read? Who do you read with?"

During the story, stop at page 8. Ask, "What is an ax and a sax? What clues does the book give Tim to help him to understand?"

After the story ask, "How did Tom feel at the beginning, middle and end of the story? How do you know?"

CHEETAH® train loves a song, zooming as it hums along.
A fox relaxes in a box. Alex wears his T-Rex socks.
Can you guess which sound is next?

Find an instrument, then play and sing along using the lyrics above!

Make our sound at the back of your mouth.

X is on the way to town.
CHEETAH® train is slowing down.

Look at the pictures, say the word and (circle) the correct spelling.

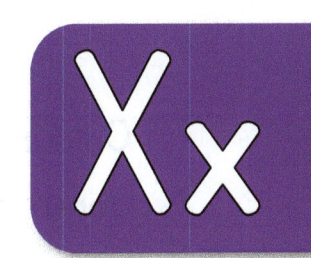

Xx

bax
box

axe
oxe

tacksy
taxi

Practise writing the letter *x*.

Excellent!

Listen and underline all the words in the passage with the /x/ sound.

In Dexter's box there was a mix of things.

He found a little axe, a toy ox, and a wax candle.

"This mix is so fun!" Dexter exclaimed.

"Every day I find something new to put in my box."

Colour the face that shows how you feel about the /x/ sound.

- Got it!
- Almost got it
- No, didn't get it

Remember to look back at the section if you are not sure you understand.

Dear Parent: Date: _____

_____ does/does not fully understand the phonic sound /x/. Please continue to review at home.

Signed: _____

Dear Teacher: Date:_____

Thank you. We have reviewed the phonic sound /x/ together. My child had a chance to teach me.

Signed: _____

Reward sticker for parent or guardian goes here.

Great job!

_____
(write name)

understands the phonic sound /x/.

Sticker for pupil goes here!

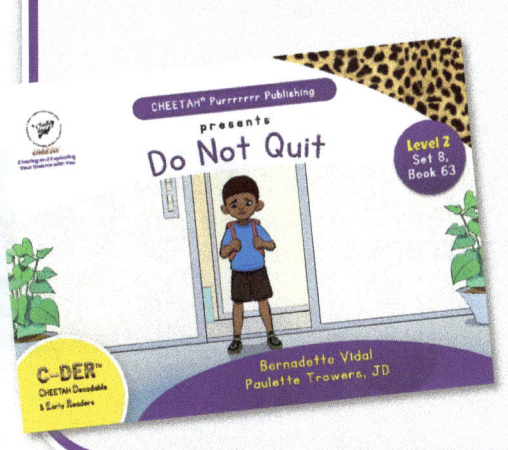

Let's read together: Do Not Quit

Before you begin, explain what it means to quit. Share a story with the child of a time you wantd to quit something.

During the story ask, "What is it that Quincy wants to quit? Why does he not like school? How does he feel?"

After the story ask, "Why does Quincy not quit school? Can you share a story of a time you wanted to quit something?"

CHEETAH® train loves a song, zooming as it hums along. In the sea is Quincy squid, swimming quickly to Madrid. Can you guess which sound is next?

Find an instrument, then play and sing along using the lyrics above!

How do you move your mouth to make our sound?

QU is on the way to town.
CHEETAH® train is slowing down.

Draw lines to match the qu words to the pictures.

squeeze   squid   quiet   queen

qu

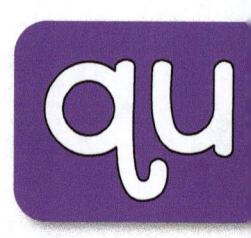

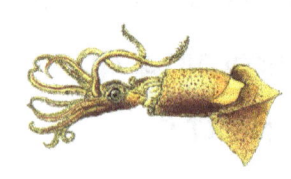

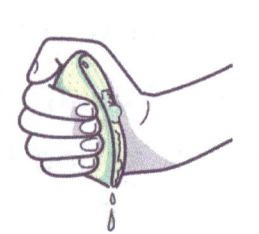

Practise writing the letters *q* and *u*.

Great job!

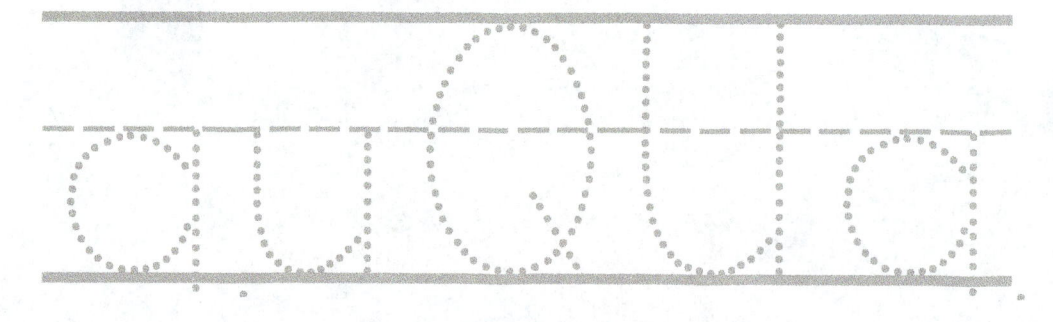

Listen and underline all the words in the passage with the /qu/ sound.

In the blue sea, a quick squid named Quinn played.

"How do you know I am a squid?" Quinn would ask.

"Because you can squirt ink!"

Said the Queen Snapper with a wink.

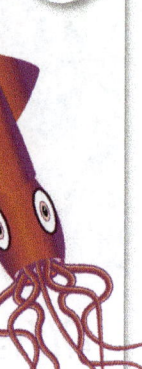

Colour the face that shows how you feel about the /qu/ sound.

😊 Got it!   😐 Almost got it   ☹ No, didn't get it

Thank you for trying. Always put your best foot forward.

Dear Parent: Date: _____

_____ does/does not fully understand the phonic sound /qu/. Please continue to review at home.

Signed: _____

Dear Teacher: Date: _____

Thank you. We have reviewed the phonic sound /qu/ together. My child had a chance to teach me.

Signed: _____

Reward sticker for parent or guardian goes here.

Amazing!

_____
(write name

understands the phonic sound /qu/.

Sticker for pupil goes here!

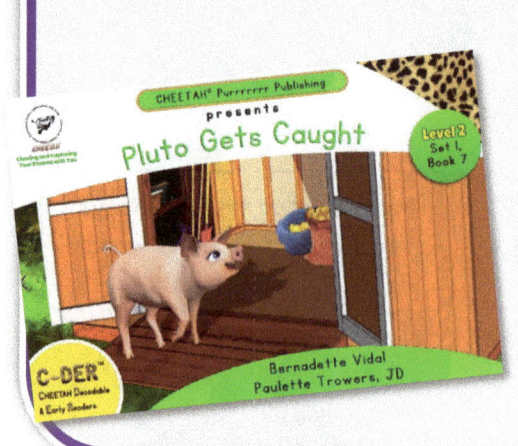

Let's read together: Pluto Gets Caught

Before you begin ask, *"Who is Pluto? What do you think will happen to them in this story? Why do you think that?"*

During the story ask, *"What is the setting for this story? How do you know?"*

After the story ask, *"Is this story realistic or fantasy? What about the story makes you think that?"*

CHEETAH® train loves a song, zooming as it hums along.
A noisy tortoise shouts hello! His voice is very loud, you know.
Can you guess which sound is next?

Find an instrument, then play and sing along using the lyrics above!

Can you make our sound three times?

OI is on the way to town.
CHEETAH® train is slowing down.

oi

Listen as an adult says the words. Tick to show if the /oi/ sound is at the start, in the middle or at the end of the word.

☐ start	☐ start	☐ start	☐ start
☐ middle	☐ middle	☐ middle	☐ middle
☐ end	☐ end	☐ end	☐ end

Practise writing the letters *oi*.

You can do this!

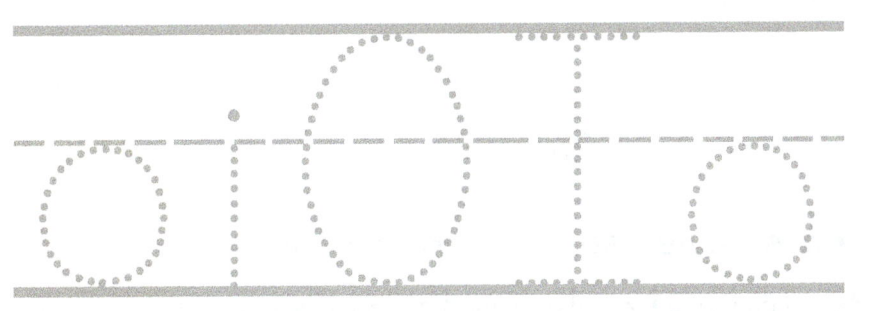

Listen and underline all the words in the passage with the /oi/ sound.

At home, there was a choice to make.

"Which oil should we use?" asked Dad.

"Would you enjoy using the olive oil?"

"Yes!" the boy said. "But does oil spoil?"

Colour the face that shows how you feel about the /oi/ sound.

Got it!   Almost got it   No, didn't get it

You are a CHEETAH, a future leader. Come, let us continue.

Dear Parent: Date: _____

_____ does/does not fully understand the phonic sound oi. Please continue to review at home.

Signed: _____

Dear Teacher: Date:_____

Thank you. We have reviewed the phonic sound /oi/ together. My child had a chance to teach me.

Signed: _____

Reward sticker for parent or guardian goes here.

Outstanding!

_____
(write name

understands the phonic sound /oi/.

Sticker for pupil goes here!

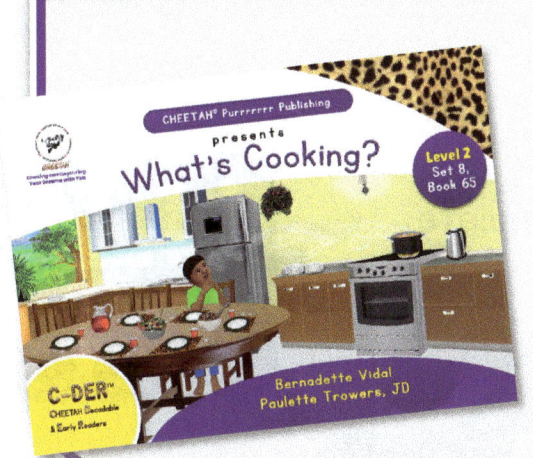

Let's read together: What's Cooking?

Before you begin ask, *"Who cooks in your home? What do they like to cook? Do you ever help them?"*

During the story ask, *"Who is telling this story? How do you know?"*

After the story ask, *"What is the lesson you should learn from this story?"*

CHEETAH® train loves a song, zooming as it hums along.
Jules the mule is very cute, playing music with her flute.
Can you guess which sound is next?

Find an instrument, then play and sing along using the lyrics above!

What shape is your mouth as you make my sound?

U is on the way to town.
CHEETAH® train is slowing down.

Look at the pictures. Use *u_e* or *ew* to complete each word.

u_e
ew

st _ _   t _ b _   m _ l _

Practise writing the letters *u*, *e* and *w*.

Keep it up!

u e w e u

Listen and underline all the words in the passage with the long u sound.

In June, a family had a blue day.

They wore blue and played a tune on a blue flute.

"Why is everything blue today?" asked little Lulu.

"Because it's our favourite colour!" said Mum.

Colour the face that shows how you feel about the /u/ sound.

😊 Got it!   😐 Almost got it   ☹ No, didn't get it

I am so proud of you for trying. Keep practising!

Dear Parent: Date: _____

_____ does/does not fully understand the phonic sound long /u/. Please continue to review at home.

Signed: _____

Dear Teacher: Date:_____

Thank you. We have reviewed the phonic sound long /u/ together. My child had a chance to teach me.

Signed: _____

Reward sticker for parent or guardian goes here.

You did it!

_____
(write name

understands the phonic sound long u.

Sticker for pupil goes here!

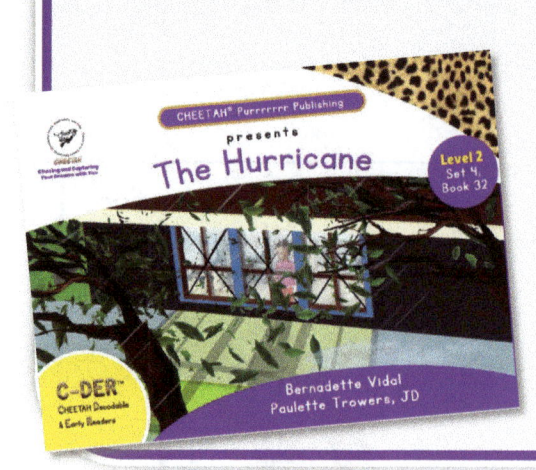

Let's read together: The Hurricane

Before you begin ask, "What is a hurricane? What do you expect to happen in this story?"

During the story, stop after page 5. Ask, "How do Jane and her Dad know the hurricane is here?"

After the story ask, "What was the big problem in this story? What did you learn about staying safe in a hurricane?"

CHEETAH® train loves a song, zooming as it hums along. Harvey wants to see the stars, and one day learn to play guitar. Can you guess which sound is next?

Find an instrument, then play and sing along using the lyrics above!

Open your mouth to make our sound.

E is on the way to town.
CHEETAH® train is slowing down.

Listen as an adult says the words. Circle the words with the /ar/ sound.

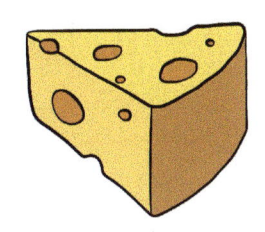

ar

Practise writing the letters *a* and *r*.

You can do this!

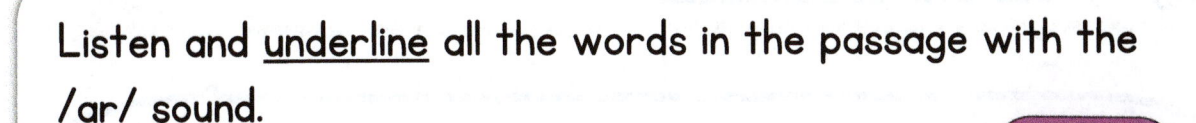

ar AR ar

Listen and underline all the words in the passage with the /ar/ sound.

Clara loves art; it is a part of her heart.

She drew a car, a star and a guitar.

Art makes her happy, right from the start.

It is a smart way to show who you are.

Colour the face that shows how you feel about the /ar/ sound.

😊 Got it!   😐 Almost got it   ☹️ No, didn't get it

You are a CHEETAH, a future leader. Come, let us continue.

Dear Parent: Date: _____

_____ does/does not fully understand the phonic sound /ar/. Please continue to review at home.

Signed: _____

Dear Teacher: Date: _____

Thank you. We have reviewed the phonic sound /ar/ together. My child had a chance to teach me.

Signed: _____

Reward sticker for parent or guardian goes here.

Keep it up!

_____
(write name)

understands the /ar/.

Sticker for pupil goes here!

CHEETAH®'s review

Write a rhyming word for each noun. Then, compare your words with a classmate and add their words!

Noun	Rhyming word	Classmate's word
join		
mix		
car		
tune		
quick		

Challenge yourself! Write a funny story with 5 of your rhyming words from above.

Use the letters to make as many ar words as you can. Letters can be used more than once, and nonsense words are welcome. Be creative and have fun!

CHEETAH®'s review

Write four words from the word box that rhyme.
Cross out the words you use.

1. _____ 2. _____
3. _____ 4. _____

Write four words from the word box that rhyme.
Cross out the words you use.

1. _____ 2. _____
3. _____ 4. _____

Write the words that remain. Draw a box around the word part (2 letters) they all share.

1. _____ 2. _____
3. _____

Word Box

coil
part
mix
tart
foil
fix
boil
dart
spoil
chart

Write a complete sentence with a word from the word box. Remember to start your sentence with a capital letter and end with punctuation! (. ? !)

_____

Find the sight words in the wordsearch.

n	y	o	u	r	y
y	u	r	s	t	o
r	a	y	e	y	u
a	r	o	u	n	d
d	e	n	c	u	e

you   use   your   are   around

CHEETAH®'s review

Make words with the oil family.

coil   _ oil

_ oil   _ oil

Use the letters from the box to make words with the long u sound.

| t | b | c | l | s |

_ u _ e   u _ e

_ u _ e   _ u e

Make words using the letters /qu/.

quick   qu_ _

qu_ _   _ _ _ _

CHEETAH® Purrrrrrr Publishing

presents

The Tune in the Park

Set 8

x, qu, oi, long u,

CHEETAH® Poster Story

1. "Quick! Get your toy shark, Joy. Time to get Hue from the park."

2. Joy rode in the car with her toy shark.

3. At the park, the sun set at six.

4. "Where is Hue?" said her mom. "It is dark."

5. Joy took the shark in her arms.

6. Then from the dark came a far quack.

JamDER™

CHEETAH Toys & More, LLC, Copyright© 2023.
All rights reserved. 876-909-6311 (WhatsApp),

The Tune in the Park

CHEETAH® Poster Story

7. Then came a bark. Again a quick quack.

8. A duck and a dog sang a cute song.

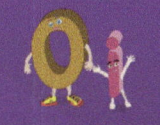

9. Then came a fox with a tune on a sax.

10. Joy and her shark gave coins to the fox.

11. Joy saw a boy wave his arm at the fox.

12. "Look, that boy is Hue!" said Joy. "Time to quit the park!"

13. In the car, Joy and Hue sang a tune to the shark.

Let's create

Complete the table. Put the letters together to make words.

beginning sound	middle sound	end sound	words created
x	a	t	
		g	
qu	e	p	
		r	
t	i	m	
		n	
r	o	w	

List the words that you do not know the meaning of.

_____

_____

Ask an adult what they mean.

Let's put together

Connect the boxes to make words from the -ar word family. Write them in the given space.

c
b   _ar   _____
f   _____
j   _____
                   _____

Create a poster of words in the -est word family.

Let's take apart

Break each word into sounds. Write the sounds in the boxes.

How many letters and phonemes do these words have?

Let's trace

Trace the letters to write sentences.

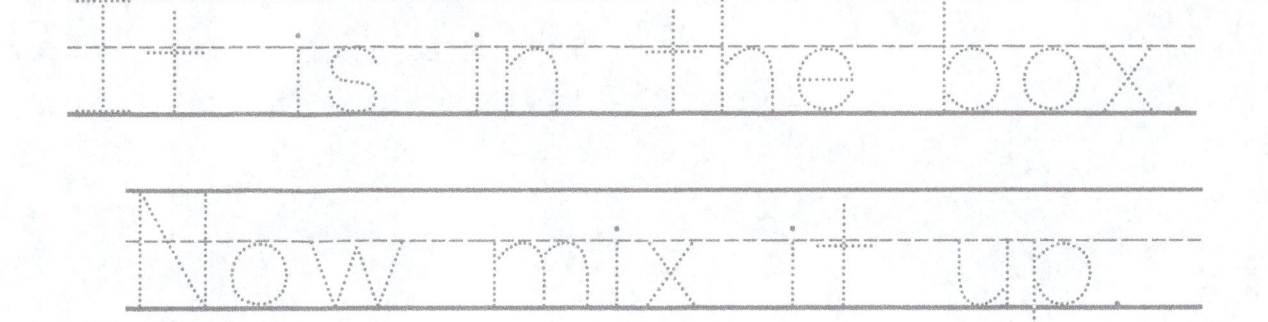

It is in the box.

Now mix it up.

Read the sentences you have written.

According to a famous Black woman, Oprah Winfrey, "Education is the key to unlocking the world, a passport to freedom." What do you think this means? Let's soar to the next page!

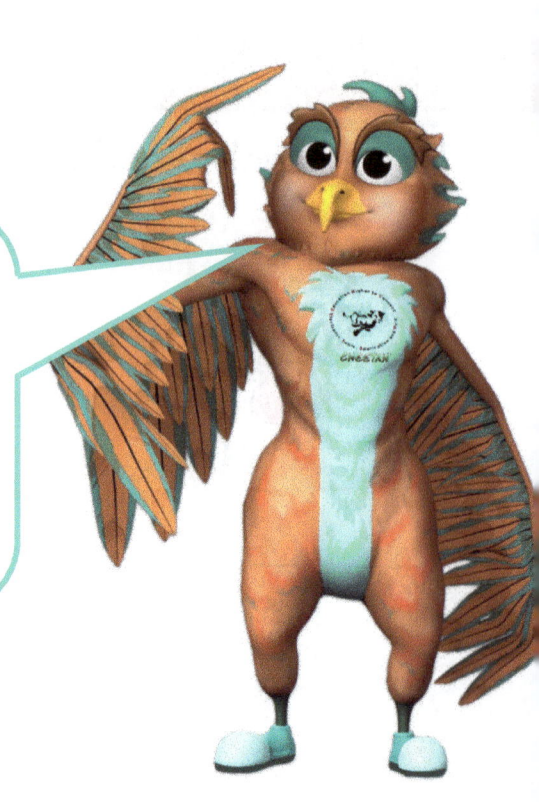

CHEETAH® reward stickers

This page is left blank
so you can cut out the reward
stickers.

Set 9

ow, ou, er, soft c and zh

Here are some JamDER books to read:

Sound	JamDER reference	Book title
ou	Set 5, Book 38	*Monkey Helps Out*
er	Set 6, Book 51	*Nature's Walk*
soft c	Set 2, Book 11	*Let Us Exercise*

5+

Set 9: /x/, /qu/, /oi/, long /u/ and /ar/

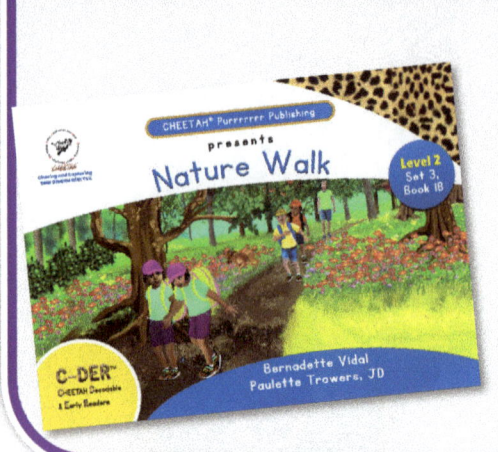

Let's read together: Nature Walk

Before you begin ask, "What is nature? What clues are there in the illustration to help us with what the word means?"

During the story, stop part way. Ask, "Do you have any questions about what we have read so far?"

After the story ask, "What happens in this story? How do the characters feel at the beginning, middle and end?"

CHEETAH® train loves a song, zooming as it hums along. Here comes Mr Brown the clown. He's wearing such a silly gown. Can you guess which sound is next?

Find an instrument, then play and sing along using the lyrics above!

How do your lips move as you make our sound?

OW is on the way to town.
CHEETAH® train is slowing down.

Listen as an adult reads the words. Write the correct word from the box under the picture.

ow

| crown | owl | flower | towel |

Practise writing the letters *ow*.

Wow! You're doing well!

Listen and <u>underline</u> all the words in the passage with the ow sound.

In the park, there was a pretty flower.

It grew upon a big brown tower.

"Now how can we get it down?" asked the clown.

He went off to get the biggest ladder in town.

Colour the face that shows how you feel about the /ow/ sound.

😊 Got it!   😐 Almost got it   ☹ No, didn't get it

Yes. You are looking much better. Keep practising! Never let it rest.

Dear Parent: Date: _____

_____ does/does not fully understand the phonic sound /ow/. Please continue to review at home.

Signed: _____

Dear Teacher: Date:_____

Thank you. We have reviewed the phonic sound /ow/ together. My child had a chance to teach me.

Signed: _____

Reward sticker for parent or guardian goes here.

Well done!

_____
(write name

understands the phonic sound /ow/.

Sticker for pupil goes here!

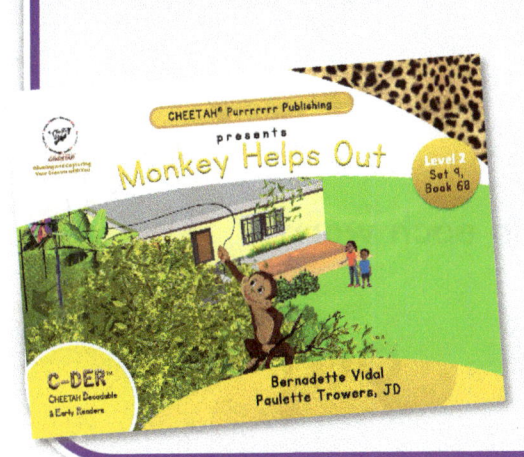

Let's read together: Monkey Helps Out

Before you begin ask, "Do you remember this character? Can you tell me more about him?"

During the story, stop at various points to ask, "Which words on this page rhyme?"

After the story ask, "Is this how you would expect monkey to behave? Why/why not? What does this tell us about monkey?"

CHEETAH® train loves a song, zooming as it hums along. Sam and Pam have often found that people on the train are loud. Can you guess which sound is next?

Find an instrument, then play and sing along using the lyrics above!

Watch in a mirror as you make our sound!

OU is on the way to town.
CHEETAH® train is slowing down.

ou

Circle the letters that make the /ou/ sound in each word.

owl   how   out

cloud   shout   town

loud   house   cows

Practise writing the letters *o* and *u*.

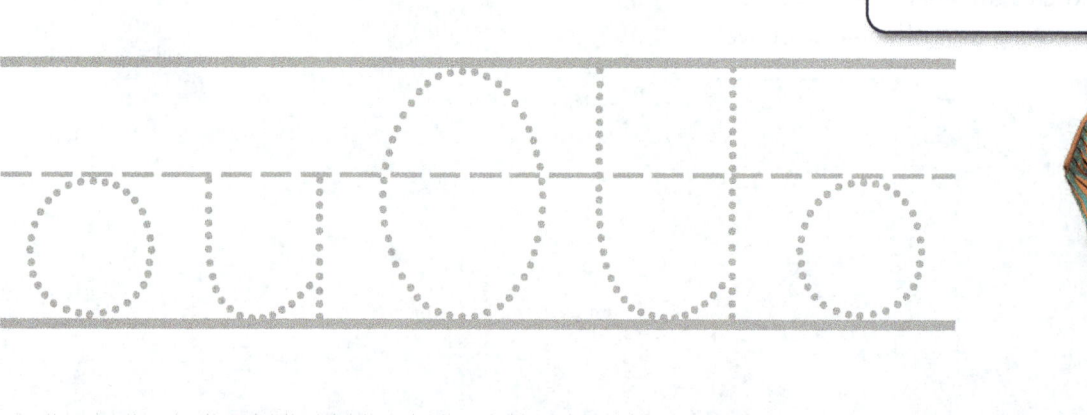

Outstanding!

ou o u o

Listen and underline all the words in the passage with the /ou/ sound.

Mouse found a big mound outside.

"This will be my new house!" he said with a smile.

He walked around and felt so proud.

His new mound was the best around.

Colour the face that shows how you feel about the /ou/ sound.

😊 Got it!   😐 Almost got it   ☹️ No, didn't get it

> Yes. You are looking much better. Keep practising! Never let it rest.

Dear Parent: Date: _____

_____ does/does not fully understand the phonic sound /ou/. Please continue to review at home.

Signed: _____

Dear Teacher: Date:_____

Thank you. We have reviewed the phonic sound /ou/ together. My child had a chance to teach me.

Signed: _____

Reward sticker for parent or guardian goes here.

You did it!

_____
(write name)

understands the phonic sound /ou/.

Sticker for pupil goes here!

Let's read together: I Like School

Before you begin ask, "Do you like school? What things do you like to do at school?"

During the story, take turns to read. Encourage the child to blend phonemes and look for clues to help with unknown words.

After the story ask, "Do you do any of the activities at school we read about in the story? Which were the same/different?"

CHEETAH® train loves a song, zooming as it hums along. The train goes under the bridge, over the hill. The afternoon is full of thrills! Can you guess which sound is

Find an instrument, then play and sing along using the lyrics above!

Open your mouth to make our sound.

ER is on the way to town.
CHEETAH® train is slowing down.

Listen as an adult reads the words. Write the missing letters to complete each word.

er ir ur

tig__

b__d

f__

Practise writing the letters *e* and *r*.

You keep getting better!

erRe

Listen and underline all the words in the passage with the /er/ sound.

In a big town, there was a tall tower.

At the top, grew a single blue flower.

"It is a flower with power," said a bird flying over it.

Everyone looked up and gave a loud cheer.

Colour the face that shows how you feel about the /er/ sound.

😊 Got it!   😐 Almost got it   ☹ No, didn't get it

You are flying high! Keep going!

Dear Parent: Date: _____

_____ does/does not fully understand the phonic sound /er/. Please continue to review at home.

Signed: _____

Dear Teacher: Date:_____

Thank you. We have reviewed the phonic sound /er/ together. My child had a chance to teach me.

Signed: _____

Reward sticker for parent or guardian goes here.

Nice job!

_____
(write name)

understands the phonic sound /er/.

Sticker for pupil goes here!

Let's read together: Let Us Exercise

Before you begin ask, "*How do people exercise? How do you like to exercise? Who do you like to exercise with?*"

During the story, stop after page 10. Ask, "*Do you think it is a good idea for Pam to join in? What might happen next?*"

After the story ask, "*What did Sam and Bella learn? What do you think they will do differently next time they exercise?*"

CHEETAH® train loves a song, zooming as it hums along.
Artist Macy loves this place, and with her pencil draws a face.
Can you guess which sound is next?

Find an instrument, then play and sing along using the lyrics above!

Feel the air leave your mouth as you make my sound.

C is on the way to town.
CHEETAH® train is slowing down.

Draw lines to match the words to the pictures.

mice   dance   city   rice

Cc

Practise writing the letter c.

Take your time.
Do your best.

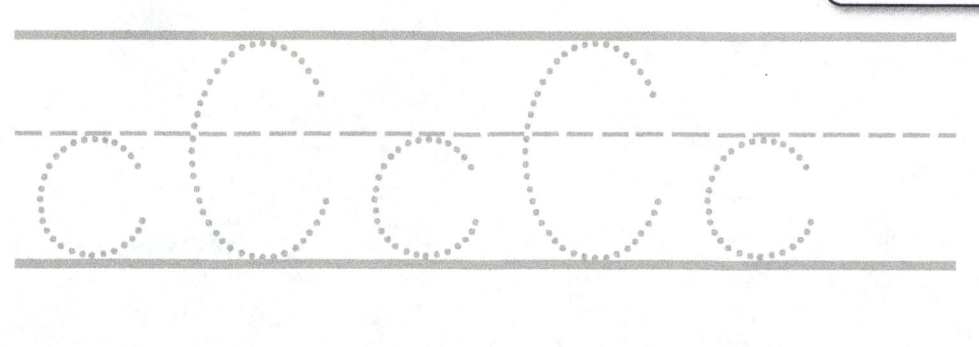

Listen and circle all the words in the passage with the soft /c/ sound.

Tracy was an ace space pilot.

She raced through space in a fancy spaceship.

She flew in circles with a smile on her face.

Tracy said that space was the best place.

Colour the face that shows how you feel about the soft /c/ sound.

😊 Got it!   😐 Almost got it   ☹️ No, didn't get it

You are doing good. Keep practising and you will reach your best.

Dear Parent: Date: _____

_____ does/does not fully understand the phonic sound soft c. Please continue to review at home.

Signed: _____

Dear Teacher: Date:_____

Thank you. We have reviewed the phonic sound soft c together. My child had a chance to teach me.

Signed: _____

Reward sticker for parent or guardian goes here.

Super effort!

_____
(write name)

understands the phonic sound soft c.

Sticker for pupil goes here!

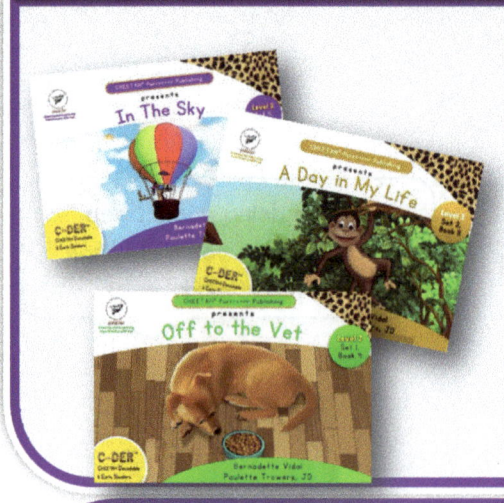

Let's read together: revisit a JamDER book of your choice!

Before you begin ask, "Why did you choose this book? Can you tell me more about it?"

Read the book together, emphasising the correct use of the conventions of print (directionality, return sweep).

After the story, ask the child direct recall questions, encouraging them to look back in the book for evidence to support their answer.

CHEETAH® train loves a song, zooming as it hums along. It zooms across the land, past elephants and yellow sand. Can you guess which sound is next?

Find an instrument, then play and sing along using the lyrics above!

Feel your vocal cords vibrate as you make our sound!

ZH is on the way to town.
CHEETAH® train is slowing down.

Listen as an adult says the words. Circle the pictures with /zh/.

su
si

Practise writing the letters s, u and i.

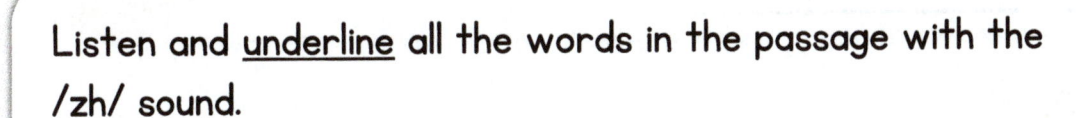

Great Job!

sisusisu

Listen and underline all the words in the passage with the /zh/ sound.

Tim found a map with a big red cross.

"I will measure the distance!" he said to his boss.

When he found the spot, he felt such pleasure.

Tim dug down and there was the treasure.

Colour the face that shows how you feel about the /zh/ sound.

😊 Got it!   😐 Almost got it   ☹ No, didn't get it

Congratulations! Great job!

Dear Parent: Date: _____

_____ does/does not fully understand the phonic sound /zh/. Please continue to review at home.

Signed: _____

Dear Teacher: Date: _____

Thank you. We have reviewed the phonic sound /zh/ together. My child had a chance to teach me.

Signed: _____

Reward sticker for parent or guardian goes here.

Fantastic!

_____
(write name

understands the phonic sound /zh/.

Sticker for pupil goes here!

CHEETAH®'s review

Look at the pictures. Choose a pair of letters from the word box that goes with the focus sound for each picture.

| su | ce | ir |

___   ___   ___

| ur | si | ce |

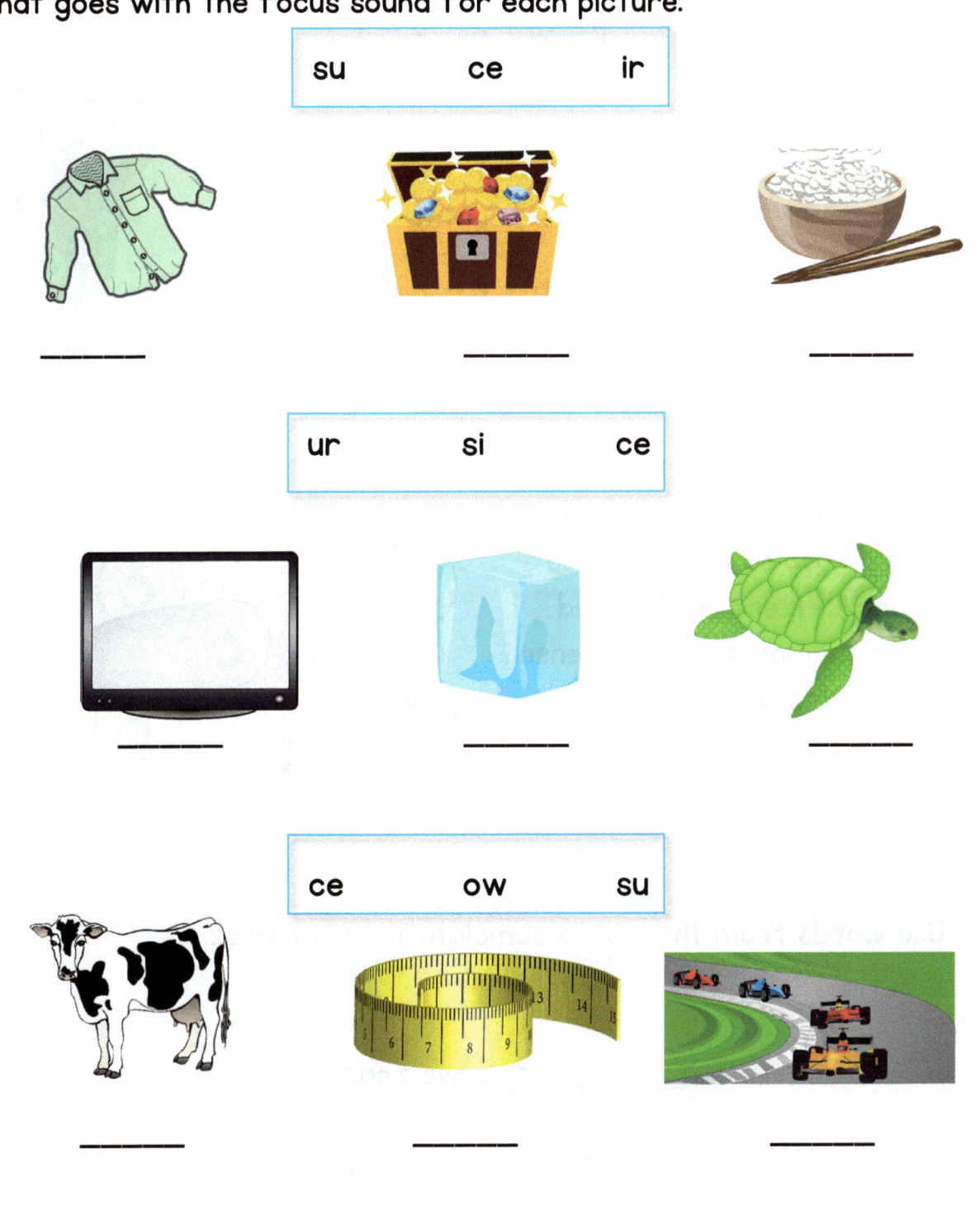

___   ___   ___

| ce | ow | su |

___   ___   ___

CHEETAH®'s review

Find the sight words in the wordsearch.

f	w	e	k	f
o	e	t	n	r
u	r	y	o	u
r	e	k	w	t
t	h	e	r	e

were   you   know   there   four

Use the letters to make as many ow/ou words as you can. Letters can be used more than once, and nonsense words are welcome. Be creative and have fun!

d e c
 o o
l h p

Use words from the box to complete the sentences.

_____ have feathers.

When we freeze water, we make _____.

Let us go shopping in _____.

cows   town   fur   ice   birds

CHEETAH® Purrrrrrr Publishing presents
Wow, Owls!

Set 9 — ow, ou, er (ir, ur)

CHEETAH® Poster Story

1. This is Miss Bird. She is the town teacher.

2. Miss Bird has a room full of owls.

3. "You can turn to an owl to chat. But do not shout."

4. The owls perch around Miss Bird.

5. The owls hoot with their mouths. They are not loud.

6. "Now, owls," says Miss Bird. Each owl in my room is a winner!"

CHEETAH Toys & More, LLC, Copyright© 2023.
All rights reserved. 876-909-6311 (WhatsApp),

Wow, Owls!

CHEETAH® Poster Story

7. "Owl, you are a quick runner! You, owl, are a good kicker."

8. "Am I a winner?" says a third owl.

9. "Yes, you can whirl!"

10. This owl is a good surfer. This bird is a singer.

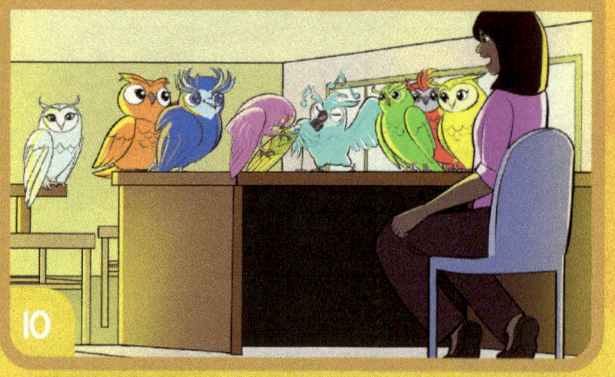

11. This girl is a born leader!

12. Wow, owls! Take a bow.

"Now, tell me. Which owl is a good reader?"

Let's create

Complete the table. Put the letters together to make words.

beginning sound	middle sound	end sound	words created
p	e	t	
	ee	g	
f	ea	p	
	o	r	
r	oo	w	
	ou	d	
c		s	

List the words that you do not know the meaning of.

_____

_____

Ask an adult what they mean.

Let's put together

Connect the boxes to make words from the _ice word family. Write them in the given space.

r
d
m
h

_ice

_____
_____
_____
_____

Can you think of words that belong to the -ow word family?

Let's take apart

Break each word into sounds. Write the sounds in the boxes.

Let's trace

Trace the letters to write sentences.

> Check that you have written each phoneme the correct way.

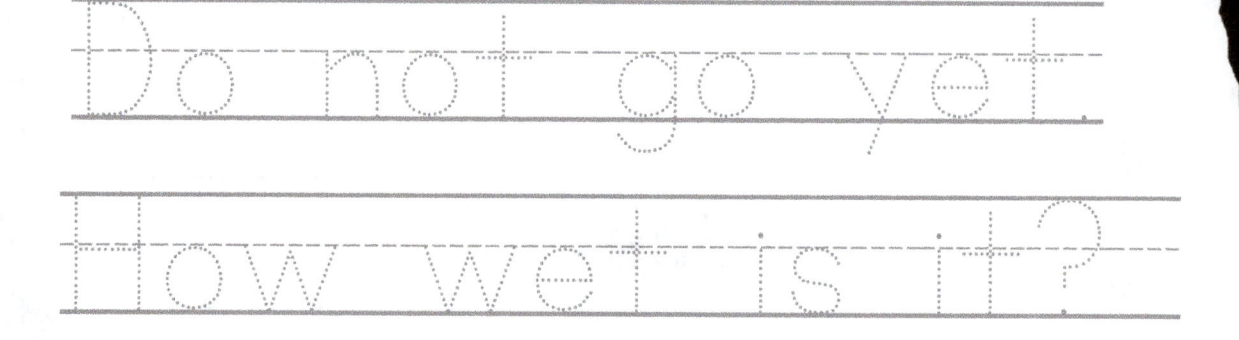

Do not go yet.

How wet is it?

Read the sentences you have written.

CHEETAH® reward stickers

This page is left blank
so you can cut out the reward
stickers.